Moth In The Fist

Verse

by

Ron Sanders

Moth In The Fist

Copyright 2008

by

Ron Sanders

ISBN: 978-0-6151-9573-5

all rights reserved
including
covers, text content, and original formatting.

ronsandersartofprose@yahoo.com

ronsandersatwork.com

Moth In The Fist

Faces

earth to Earth

Sweet Illusion

The Rabid Angel

Ascent

Faces

Black is the seed, and black, the fruit.

The blossom of light an affront: wrought of nothing,
resolving nothing, returning to nothing—the blossom is
Everything.
    And a man contends, endures,
knowing, in his moment, that all that matters
matters not; that in the crowd
he is alone, that in the cosmos
he is lost, that in his writing
he is written. He is a coal, shot hot between voids.
    Intense to evanescent, each pass of a life
has a spectrum.

Red is the womb.

Here, at riot's eye, all bellows howl,

all fires bend to the harlot wind of becoming.

And the nub is a lump, and the lump *accrues,*

marbles dreamless, in liquor weightless, defining:

Liquid ruby, clinging vine, tallow flower in wine—

the little ogre, caught on a briar, kicks.

Comes a marvelous trophy, born squirming and gory,

torn naked and pendent, borne blind and grotesque—

wound about the hollows and seams, spat in a maelstrom:

    one more shape in the window, one more shadow exposed

    in the bloody triumph of light.

Out of the whirl, the faces gather round.

The boy has opened his eyes,

but the infant makes no sound.

    Shapes loom to the sides, to the front and rear:

    The faces grin, closing in . . . grow enormous fingers

    to point, to pinch—to peel back the veil

    and make his eyes scream.

    In the dimness a glimmer, a nimbus, a pearl.

The colors peak. Within their arms a becking form appears.

    The figure is a woman, whose seeming lips recite:

        "Come sunder the night. Little ember, ignite.

        I am mother, I am mother. I am life, I am light."

But like oil on a rainy day,

the colors blend and wend their way

into the whirl, and there,

subdued, the voice is slurred,

the light, obscured,

and night

renewed.

Here on the lattice,

morning embroiders the tatters of night.

While tall beaded glasses

squeeze melody from melting ice,

the diced and slanting shafts of sun

checker the shadows with tangerine light.

> *On the sidewalks April's children run*
>
> *but the eyes in the faces see*
>
> *nephew on the august perch*
>
> *of uncle's wicker knee.*

Graven in air, the faces shift,

their eyes a flickering stream.

Loosed features drift, expressions run

in subtle strokes of shade and sun.

The stream sucks him in: swirls of abhorrence,

pools of disdain. Succumbing, drawn under,

he swallows his eyes. But the eyes in the faces remain

watching.

So scrawny it grieves, he eats too damned much.

Ever absent, he is always in the way.

Sickly, quiet, submissive, shy,

he hides when the faces quarrel,

cries when they crack his lie.

Craving love, he learns early to fast.

Contriving a limp, he is weaned at last.

What hold wanders here—there are no bridges,

only walls. Every scribe is a master of cant.

The learned are jaundiced, the ignorant smug,

and those who would name his demons,

when maintaining, "this will pass,"

fashion their webs of pap and straw.

This animal man is a thief.

Mother,

My world is a stranger. My eyes are wounds
on a mind that will not heal.
I saw more range, more warmth, more *mother,*
in the dance of sun on heather,
in a single kiss of dew.
Now your urn, blessed bowel, fouls the cedar
of father's mantel, while he grows blacker,
blending bile with grief and gin.
Those lips that never tendered,
that heart I never knew—mother,
who *were* you?

Ubiquitous, the emerald slut lies splayed, exploding:
from her pores an eruption, on her belly a rank,
stinking moss. She bleeds life, vomits it,
into bud, into blade; sharing with a passing star
the silent scream of spring.
    But here she dreams, perfumed,
    a picture of grace, her verdure in groom.
    Secluded, seduced, sedated. Churls put on her face
    while zephyrs attend to the scent of her loom.
Time purls. The zephyrs flit sweetly,
chasing motes in fibers of light.
Playing tag in the sun, currents weave into one
near a still-life of mourners and fatherless son.
The figures seem rooted, unreal. As the gust musses trees
    light leaps between leaves. The greenery breathes.
    As if shaken the scene comes to life.
Huddling in sync, the faces incline, their eyes
like slinking thieves – the young man implodes.
The tension relents and he straightens. He wheels.
He limps off alone, wind hounding his heels,
the moment too eerie to bear. Sedans trickle by,
a raw widow grieves. But the faces continue to stare.
    And the wind pirouettes, finds a wing,
has a plunge, brakes low on a rest,
makes a guarded descent. The breeze buffets markers,
losing vigor and bent, then slips thru the stones
toward the beckoning trees.
The draft riffles leaves, where its whisper is spent
and lost as a sigh.

A stipend, a shack, a lessor in wait.
Such are the fruits of his father's estate.
He breaks no bread, seeks no sweet.
Strange dynamics govern his blood,
preclude his seed from the common fire.
Music of amity, refinement's caress,
are brute concerns; abrasive, obscene.
In his quiet aching way he is whole.

Seasons burst and smolder, surrender and brood.
Their pageant revolves about him.
The years breathe, driving the crowd,
steeping its fevers in jasmine and sun.
Humanity brawls, exalting the flame.
But without him.

And he grays, sinking, certain his pain cannot,
could not possibly, be borne by another.
The silence condenses, sets.
At last even pain deserts him.

But near the brink he hears the nervous hum
of impermanence, feels the white pang of being's wing
as day succumbs to the abyss of night.
Dawn burns deeper, duller; each beam towing
a filament of dusk, each round of the wheel a salvo
in the stunning of his eyes.

Now the years are mired in sameness.

The day wears on. Guests come unbidden:

Conscience, the despot. Sentiment, the leech.

Misgivings sojourn, transmigrate, return,

as Lonesomeness plumbs his moribund vein,

metastasizing.

Still he rooms with the wind, dies waking,

dreams sleepless. And it dogs him:

all this teeming while an instant, an irrelevancy,

a rube's view of the pulse careening downstream,

working its rhyme into a billion like irrelevancies.

      Here *must* be real, Now *must* be sound, and yet—

        no sooner are the moments cast

          than shape is shadow, and present, past.

        Only the day wears on.

Blue is the evening begotten, the twilight

of our lives. Dark gathers, mooring its stain

where a dreamer weighs the deep, his eyes in ruin,

his color in vain. Only ballast and mind,

merely ego and rind, growing blind

as the day wears on.

       Down this grim promenade

       a musty wind hustles gaunt silhouettes.

       They are loth to be borne;

       they are patiently measuring stones.

Eyes leap in their caverns, looks light and remain

on a smudge in the gloaming, a scarecrow with cane,

tapping out his tenure in a cold feeble rain.

       And now the purple veins of near-night

       thud sluggishly, almost grudgingly.

       The black earth splits wetly, obscenely.

There: *something impatient stirs, exposed.*

       Limbless, sightless, the lamprey rises;

       her breath unbearable, her length immeasurable,

       her age—impossible!

Preening whore, hypnotic.

In one vile kiss she is sieve and abyss.

Her bruised lips are splayed, her violet mouth, made,

and her churning, insatiable craw is

pitch.

Out of the whirl, the faces gather round.

Was he hurt?

Can you hear me?

But the old man makes no sound.

    Shapes loom to the sides, to the front and rear;

    The faces glare, stealing air . . . grow enormous fingers

    to prod, to pin—to pull down the veil

    and make his eyes seize.

In the dimness a glimmer, a nimbus, a pearl.

The colors peak. Within their arms a becking form appears.

The figure is a woman, whose seeming lips recite:

    "Come sunder the night. Waning fire, grow bright.

    I am mother, I am mother. I am life, I am light."

But like spectra from a dying sun,

the colors flare, are torn, are spun

into the whirl, and there,

subdued, the voice is hushed,

the blossom, crushed,

and night

renewed.

earth to Earth

settling.

The miasma pools;

notes the molten eyes, the razor breath,

tenses.

Tapering, groping, a lone probe extends;

advances wispily, tentatively, tests recoiling flesh

tenderly.

Trembling, the mass gathers, rears—

coughing.

The air like gravel,

fingers gloved in ice.

Knowing,

the old man feels his shadow tugged,

turns.

The lash rips across his cheek,

plunges,

finds the stumbling, lunatic heart,

squeezes.

Flaring, the probe bristles, dives;

severing nerve, shattering bone,

sucking furiously at marrow—

whipping the flimsy carcass about,

dashing its brittle skull on stone;

pounding it, flaying it,

sacking its means. Smashing and

gutting and

tramping and

grinding it

down.

        To gristle, to gore,

        to compost, to clay—

        onus, elan, are vent in the wind;

        the vessel dissolves

        to garbage, to grit, to whisper.

        To wit:

to seepage, to silt, to sediment

lost in the soil,

settling.

Sweet Illusion

Not to rupture the seam.

In the long ring of locking skulls

appeals to the deaf are the bones of soliloquy.

    Then like *ooze* they descend, rejoicing again!

The wise in their easy faith, their docile drift,

their wholesome lies.

By what strength do I, least pious of men,

ascend these dim flights of reason: never bending,

still I thirst; this rail—this ruse—both crutch and curse...

such a dogged ass...their cult of light could be mine!

had not that wasting disease, that mad desire to *know*,

been spawned in childhood, grown fat on my naivete

—had not that dark ogre Truth

won possession of my mind.

    I was young and strong and foolish. I held

a restless plum in granite, ripe for any man

with nerve enough to worship sense over myth.

    Their God of rust and platitudes is still

a hoax well-meant—is still beneath me.

But—I'm *older* now, and bound by time
to grip the rail, to check my climb:
each step an hour, each day a tier. Ah, to pause,
to kneel, to part with my dignity here.
Up once more. And who am I to think I'll find
the answers I've been living for.
      Let me hold my peace, never lose my grip
let me hang on till my senses slip.
Let me close to mind each skeptic's call
as death takes wing to break his fall:
      Don't leave me, dear God, not again!
      Catch me lest my life should end.

worm

As this fever is groomed for the grave,

it weathers the lash of time.

Though lamb is the morsel you crave,

your sheep perseveres into prime.

You will have your prize, but while I seethe

this mind is *mine*: I'll not be swayed

by a crude, transparent suggestion.

      I'll bind my eyes, deny I see

that gleam, that sweet illusion

dance on, seducing me.

      I'll right my spine, I'll lock my knees,

I'll cast this trembling life aloft

in offer to a breeze,

never knowing whence it rose

nor ever where it flees.

Damn you.

Each riddle answered begets *another* riddle!
Each vagabond, protean solution
is but a fragment of the boundless puzzle.
      While I have strength let me learn.
Let me juxtapose, let me correlate the pieces.
Let me vow to expose you, to hound you till I pin you down;
to rave the melancholy deep, while sane enough to see
that I'm older now, and due in time
to doubt my mind, to sense that I'm
nearly where you want me.

Beyond this feeble glow
    all is certainly darkness.
Yet the wise speak of a further life,
of a will to come. They whimper when prodded;
dogs drugged by a dream. Their gilt Dove a bauble—
like children, they are hypnotized by the gleam.
I can see it in their eyes.
And to pause here I can almost see
an endless night embracing me.

  Listen: there is mirth at the threshold,
a perverse kind of pride.
  Hypocrites! echolalics! somniloquists all!
—mother reason, make them cease. I know now
it is wrong to be right. I am lone, and ever colder.
You . . . *bitch!* Why did you banish my feet from their dance,
why must my heart want to mangle the rhyme.
  If I were a wiser man, I would plunge into Light.
  Yet I set my teeth and climb. Come worm, be swift;
  there are shimmers in the dusk.
  And I'm older.

Take these eyes
        that I may not be dazzled by lies any longer.
Break this hold, that I might extrapolate,
die born, and in my hour dare to face you:
        to brave the night, to leap the rail,
        to lift that last forbidden veil
        and make this coward see;
        to fall, to grasp the loom of time,
        to lose my mind, to sense that I'm
        nearly where you want me.

The Rabid Angel

Seems the spirit ever mends
though the light behind it bleeds.
Poor lamp am I. How strange
that the mind should sharpen
while the maggot feeds.

Each day the world grows older,
yet her face remains fair, her view serene.
I've seen the way she milks her young,
and watched her fields rush green.
But only as the sight grows weak
can at last these old eyes see
what waits the clear, unbroken pools
in wide eyes peeking back at me.

You children play, and don't mind me.
The sun lies full where I drift, content.
If I seem to be brooding on happiness spent,
then forgive me; I'm grateful
to not have to brood on sorrow.

So you children play. Can it truly be!
Did time once bend, could hurts once heal—
it seems so long . . . seems almost unreal
that I was a creature of yesterday
who could not see past the morrow.

And where is that child now?

Is he dead, was he dreamt, is he lost for good,
or is he only sleeping?
He would run, he would leap, he would laugh if he could.
He has savored his while, has lived his life to the full.
Why then is he weeping?

You children play, you children play.
Embrace this splendid, fleeting day.
But elsewhere. Look away.
Drink from the cup while the taste is sweet
and bask in the light of your youth.
Ah, what is youth but a longing for age
and age but a longing for youth.
Feel the deep pulse of summer,
the moth in the fist
—that brief, nervous fever
in a child's first kiss,
grown cold in the arms of the hunter,
matured, developed to
    this?

You children play, you children play.

The leech has yet to find you.

Let your blood sing while it may.

The rabid angel's eyes are bright,

her loving voice is lying.

The bitch can blend. And how pleasantly she stings!

All our lives we look to *things*.

I tell you, by my eyes,

there are things behind things

tending bashful children, spiteful children;

the angel lures her grateful prey,

herding awkward children, skipping children,

skipping their childhood away.

    No measured salve, no secret salt,

    no will can hold the years at bay.

All alone I watch them, day by day,

growing,

slowing in their play.

Ascent

This cycle spoken, sealed—four dark whispers
for naught, one more urgent missive to nowhere.
But I've stifled and hedged; I've danced with allusions,
found fabric in hue. One word lies mute,
one oath not thrown. Against the night
I hurl this stone, my final blasphemy:
In infinity everything reduces to nothing—
the heavens a mist, your God a blip,
all existence a freak of light and shadow.
Nothing is punier than arrogance.
    This is a clockwork universe. Yet it has no mainspring,
measures only instaneity in perpetuity.
Unseen wheels turn in thunderous silence,
building monoliths of debris, spattering flame
on a canvas boundless, artless, imponderable.
    And in this wild is a field of diamonds.
And in this field is a cult of nine. Here a fat star nests,
spinning in pitch and timelessness,
flinging slices of life on a wet little world
that pulses, thriving, forever falling
round a warm mother sun.

My world is mindblowingly beautiful.

In azure and cream the days bleed to gray.

Life bursts upon life: grace splashes in wood,

jewels tremble in brine. Shadows embark on the wind.

Every rustle and surge, each strumming of wing,

echos the rhythms of season and tide.

Again: leaf follows sun, wind scatters rain.

Streams rush to bed, to the lullaby of sea.

We are woven in time:

As we garner to sow, so we tumble to rise.

Night begets day as the sleeper dreams his eyes—

The light is on, the light is off.

The light is on, the light is off.

It is the great dissolution that gives us mountains,

the sweet swindle of hope that makes magic almost tangible.

Man posits in fragments; while he fashions and delves

still he dabbles in phantoms, transmogrifies truths.

The light is on, the light is off.

        His is a legacy of fire.

He is captor, he is hoarder, he is hero nonetheless.

And one day he will master his blood.

Somehow this wielder, this muser, this passionate beast

who worked his way from stone to steel,

will bear his pain with courage,

find his peace in forgiveness,

and rear his young with imagination.

        The light is on.

also by this author

NOVELS

Freak

(horror thriller)

Signature

(intellectual fantasy)

Microcosmia

(sweeping adventure)

Carnival

(social satire)

STORY COLLECTIONS

The Deep End

Legerdemainia

Have Pen, Will Marvel

Avainlable On Amazon